HOW TO LOVE EVERYONE
AND ALMOST
GET AWAY WITH IT

HOW TO LOVE EVERYONE
AND ALMOST
GET AWAY WITH IT

Lara Egger

UNIVERSITY OF MASSACHUSETTS PRESS
Amherst and Boston

Copyright © 2021 by University of Massachusetts Press
All rights reserved
Printed in the United States of America

ISBN 978-1-62534-571-4 (paper)

Designed by Sally Nichols
Set in Dante MT Pro and Neutra Titling
Printed and bound by Books International, Inc.

Cover design by Kristina Kachele Design, llc
Cover art: Kat Evans, *Sketchbook Page 1*, © 2019. Courtesy of the artist.
www.katevans.art.

Library of Congress Cataloging-in-Publication Data
A catalog record for this book is available from the Library of Congress.

British Library Cataloguing-in-Publication Data
A catalog record for this book is available from the British Library.

FOR MY TEACHERS

and for teachers everywhere

CONTENTS

HOW TO LOVE EVERYONE
AND ALMOST
GET AWAY WITH IT

DEAD RECKONING

I blame my recklessness on the moonquakes.
Though doctors claim otherwise, I swear

the right side of my tongue is sweeter than the left.
The truth comes with a warning label,

and some people enjoy the taste. That one day
I will confess everything should be grounds enough

for forgiveness. Who am I kidding?
All the beds on the moon are waterbeds.

To calculate one's position by way of the stars
is dead reckoning. This is the same

as opening a book of poems to a random page
and pretending the words were written for you.

During a moonquake, even the most faithful compass
points in the direction of any nearest heart.

A NEW *NEW GUIDE*

Look at this orange. When Rothko
painted No. 12, 1954, was he thinking
of a setting sun, or a piece of fruit?
In every language I know,
the word for *both* is the same.
In ancient Greek, there is no blue,
so Homer said wine-dark,
and honey was green; even the sky
stretched like a canvas above the Aegean
was cast in bronze. Sometimes, at night,
I worry about what I'm missing,
simply because I don't know the word for it.

THE IGNEOUS HOURS

Today the sun whispered another secret
into the deaf dog's ear. Page 6 of the Owner's Manual
states: *to prevent oxidization, the human shadow*
requires ten minutes of eye contact, daily,
but mentions nothing of pheromones,
and the soul's trouble-shooting page
is missing. I'm trying to remember
where it all went wrong—
maybe the day I learned the Bangles weren't singing
about *just another man named Monday,*
or the night I was mistaken for a prostitute,
and felt, for the first time, I had a shot at beauty.
In Tibetan sign language, the word *shadow*
is the same as the sign for *imaginary friend.*
In this country, just last week,
a shadow was arrested for stalking.
Permission. Redemption. As if a sunset
knows the difference. But it's true, isn't it, in those
igneous hours, anything goes.
More than once, you must have heard it:
the world is your oyster. And the deaf dog laughing,
burying the shucking knives with his bones.

DRIVING LESSONS

You are in a car driving away from ruin;
no, you are in a car, with a man, driving toward it.
A diamond sign says *dangerous curves ahead*.

The man is a good driver. He has both hands
on the wheel. He runs over ten wrong choices
without dirtying the windshield.

This could have been one of those days
you saw a bad idea on the side of the road
and ignored it. There will be a snake

curled around its dinner where you're going.
Its body will be bigger than its head.
Halfway to his house you realize

you left your wallet at home, and took
betrayal instead. But what does it matter?
The man you are with almost understands you;

one hand on the wheel, the other hand
saying nice things. You stop for gas, a pack
of mistakes, unfiltered. You see a missed call

from Mr. Practical, and hope nothing's awry.
Across the highway, the light falls at an angle
that makes the road look wet.

You are with a man who loves you.
His hands say nice things. The sign says
for once, please don't feed the animals.

ELEVEN DAYS IN ALICANTE

Night idled at the intersection of
indigo and violet; I remember
the cherry tree, studded with stars.
In that light, he was all jaguar—*listo.*

I've been dreaming about rain again.
Fishing for moonlight in the kiddie pool;
I catch a clingstone peach, a pair of pliers.

Already, I needed him to forgive me.

The word for blooming is *brotando;*
the sound, perhaps, of effort, forcing its way—

Find an expression for this.
Skin, like the smell of fortune cookies and cut grass.
In the distance, an engine of crickets, humming.

My car is adrift on the ocean.
A wild animal is at the wheel. Stranger still,
in the dream, circling above us, a plane
writing *Viva Las Vegas* in the sky.

I want him   to know I'm sorry.

Brotando: by definition, sprout, burst forth, grow quickly but
in context, as between us,
blooming: flowering, budding, opening—
glowing, as with vigor,
as with pain.

Morning broke at the junction of cowardice
and ruin; the moon dissolved
on the tongue of the sky. Had we slept at all?
In that light, all angel—*tremendo.*

He dreamed my hair was on fire and there was no one to
    put it out.

Consider the cherry tree; how its buds wrestle
against what tries to contain them.
There is no expression for this.

S.O.S.

Mondays the heart needs a parachute;
Tuesdays, a life jacket.
This man's is black and blue.
Despite the heartburn, we volunteer
to walk through Calamity's revolving door.
Ask the blind baseball team,
the headless orchestra—
do you really need all five senses?
To hear a dog dreaming
is to understand the anguish of clouds.
To lie to oneself is inevitable.
Raise your hand if you're willing
to break the bad news
to the music-box ballerina.
In some languages, *flamenco* is an anagram
of *arrhythmia. Tachycardia*
is the sound as the sole hits the floor.
An octopus has three hearts
but uses none of them.
The woman with three arms
rarely pays for her own drinks.
Sometimes the gods mistake our shipwrecks
for symphonies; we try to sink
the melody but the melody
always swims.

WANDERLUST

Today I put my heart in an envelope
and mailed it into the world.

Like yours, it has a bucket list.
There's an antidote for every poison

except regret, its bite deadlier than five King Cobras'.
To avoid it, I once threw my heart

into the Dead Sea. To avoid it, I've occasionally
mistaken risk for chance.

It's noon, and the moon is still loitering around
like an awkward conversation.

Before you mail your heart into the world,
it's advisable to calculate the odds of its return:

x being the hopelessness of a hot-air balloon,
divided by quadratic y, the crocodile's congenitally

hungry leer. My father taught me this equation.
Mother never forgave him.

Did you know, across the international dateline,
there's a village where adulterers

are believed to be earthly manifestations of god?
I've been there. I kissed a man

until my mouth became a conch shell of secrets.
Even at sunrise, the village's feral harbor

was already thinking about dinner.
Don't you think the difference between discretion

and deception is mostly academic? If it comes back,
my heart will declare nothing but a vow of silence.

THE ONE-HIT WONDERS

Someone let the bobcat out of the bag—was it you?
It's okay if you prefer to remain anonymous.
The delta between heroism and hubris
is mostly silence, as in, silently each morning
the gods jumpstart our souls, adjusting the mirrors
toward astonishment. Believe it or not,
the scientific term for a group of flamingos
is a *flamboyance;* believe it or not, there's a word—
gynotikolobomassophile—for someone who enjoys
nibbling on the lobes of a woman's ear.
In 1983, Matthew Wilder had a hit with "Break My Stride"
but when he gave his name at a Starbucks last week,
no one turned their heads, even though the song
was playing in the background, even though
the cashier would hum its tune under her breath
for the rest of her shift. The universe is full
of one-hit wonders. Am I a one-hit wonder?
Did I leave my decency in the wrong man's bed?
Between dinner and dessert, there's always room
for another miracle. Some nights a fog
disappears the hills, then lifts by daybreak
with the stealth of a magician's handkerchief.

IF YOU'RE ANYTHING LIKE ME

You've imagined how it feels to have a magician
saw you in half. Sorry, these exit seats are already taken.
The irises I planted were every audacity
of bruise, and still you said they were ravishing.
There are healthy ways to enjoy a relationship
with pain. Glitter glue, for example.

Sometimes I fall in love with the wrong words.
Yesterday, I walked around the kitchen saying
xylophone, xylophone, xylophone, when what I really needed
was a particle accelerator good with maps.
Nothing changes. Then it does. Who's taking minutes?
I want to know why my fingerprint looks

like dishwater circling a drain. I want to know why angels
form a V, and not a circle, when they fly.
If you're anything like me, you've asked yourself:
is the future more like a fossil or a carnival claw
vending machine? When I talk about pain
I mean these irises, frostbitten overnight.

A NEW *NEW GUIDE* TO HEREDITY

The Australians and the Japanese have collaborated
to genetically engineer a blue rose. The experiment has failed.
The rose is lavender (itself another thing)
with an aura at its edges that looks glassblower blue.

STILLE NACHT

My father accompanied our carols
with his accordion. He was a guitar man at heart.

The case's plush crimson lining seemed almost
too considerate for the heft and moan of the thing

collecting dust in the corner between nativities.
If you look too closely at the moon, it will blind you;

I've learned the hard way, if you think there's always honor
in truth, *silence* waits on its altar.

The accordion is the perfect instrument for someone
who descended from a line of executioners,

its bellows modeled on the efficiency of the guillotine.
One Christmas, snooping for gifts, I found a letter

from my father's lover. His secret bloomed in me.
Ripe fruit crystalized and hungry indecencies.

While Mother sugarcoated the *Lebkuchen,*
Dad strapped the instrument around my shoulders.

He taught me how to press the buttons
and squeeze at the same time.

DRUNKEST ETC.

It is a choice between fire and ice,
between the Cowardly Lion and Puss in Boots,
between the word and the flesh
and the doubt in the middle.
Blake said it best, desire should be
unstoppable, not a choice: Rice Krispies
or Cocoa Puffs, the baby or the freedom
of the bath, not a deliberation on keeping
the airplane blanket or not.
Research suggests: all-you-can-eat buffets
increase the likelihood of infidelity.
It has been ten years since you looked at yourself
naked. You take piano lessons
because you think it will make you
more attractive. In some countries
it is illegal to be yourself.
After coffee and bagels, your mother admits
she has never been in love.
Did John Prentice and Joey stay together?
The neighbor's dog has died,
and even though she wasn't yours,
you feel like you might have lost
the one living creature who understands you.
Your friend tells a joke about raping
a unicorn. Somewhere there's a picture of you,
doing the right thing.

AT WASHINGTON SQUARE TAVERN

How astonishing it is that desire always remembers,
and terrifying that its memory is often flawed. Dead, we say,
of fallen leaves, what is right, we decide, after the heart
has failed. The Spanish sing of *La Despedida*, the farewell,
but where is the necessary sadness in our language
of parting? I make a salad to hear the sound of the spoons
ring like church bells against the bowl. I fall into the abyss
and learn to love it, wondering if it thinks of itself
as interminable, wondering if it goes by any other name—
gulf, chasm, void—the difference as subtle, subjective,
as the way you slide the toothpick from your martini glass
and graze it across my outstretched palm. My vision of you
can be expressed by a pasture of nervous horses. My hope
is a sea anemone, panning light on the ocean floor. O God!
If this recklessness was an ancient civilization, would it leave
pyramids or corpses in its wake? And would scholars, upon
deciphering the hieroglyphs of my love, discover blossoms
or only scars? We meet each other here, in the darkness
of this bar, where fidelity is the first of our surrenders.
We are not too old. We still have time. What we want the most
should never be touched. We are not yet dead, just falling.

THE BRIDGE BETWEEN US

If there was trouble,
            we entered willingly.
    We sharpened the day
                into glass. Somewhere
a bell rang. Somewhere a bird flew its desire
            into the open mouth of the world.
         We reached for it.
                Or maybe it fell.

What if
      what lands between two people
isn't destiny after all,
         but simply the body mistaking
    another's orbit for its own,
          the course of things
no more sacred than the names we give them?

         You once said the difference
between a lightning bug and a firefly
      could be measured
           by their weight
        in the palm of your hand.

Close your fist, then, tell me—
    how light,
      when held tightly enough,
          begins to burn.

MUSEUM OF THE HEART

It was the year I left my best self.

Exhibit A: the portraits of Egon Schiele:
Standing Male Nude, Black-Haired Girl with High Skirt, The Family.
It was the first of my infidelities.

> Where did you meet?
> > On the bow of a violin.
>
> What did you do there?
> > Ate birds and salted fruit.
>
> Who saw you?
> > Three caged zebra finches.

It took me no time to learn how to love two men at once
and how to lie about it. Exhibit B: my father's fountain pen:
Darling Karen, I'll say it's a business trip. I promise to leave her soon.

> Was she the only one?
> > The streets are full tonight.
>
> When did he stop?
> > Full of cats tonight.
>
> Wasn't he ashamed?
> > Their love sounds like screaming.

I have often wondered if the way we love
is hereditary. Exhibit C: a book my lover gave me:
Dear one, You are an angel.

> Were you caught?
> > Topaz for touching with caution.
>
> Did you regret it?
> > For what is mourned, Aquamarine.
>
> Who will be next?
> > Diamond, for what cannot be broken.

Exhibit D: Béla Bartók's six string quartets:
Did she forgive him?
                    Our house has many violins.
Did you forgive him?
                    I am my father's daughter.
Where is the angel?

ANOTHER VERSION OF MY CONFESSION

My affection is a tabloid on sale at register three.
Citing moral reservations, the produce section

prefers not to get involved. Even the usually forgiving
cauliflower thinks my choices are questionable.

Have you noticed how some days the rush-hour light
makes the world look as if it's snorkeling?

Stalled in the desperation of the strip-mall parking lot,
I tally my indiscretions; dog-eared romances

steadily expiring like glove-compartment coupons;
what would have been saved had I not agreed to love them?

Some nights my affection petrifies the lake,
a hush of ice tempering what lies beneath, and others,

a storm invites the water to trouble freely.
The clocks will be turned forward and then back.

Darkness falling, yet another way to describe twilight,
another way, dusk. Will you still think I'm a terrible person

if I tell you I meet emptiness everywhere, and my heart
slips easily into its pockets? Up and down the supermarket aisles,

past cold-shouldered Kleenex and tight-lipped Lean Cuisines,
past the chorus of deli cuts chanting its condemnation: my affection

is a tabloid on sale at register three. When the night manager
    closes up
he pulls last week's scandal from the rack—old stock

but his wife likes to read them. I write Catastrophe's name
in steam on the shower door. I offer to give him a ride home.

A NEW *NEW GUIDE* TO LUNAR AMBULATION

This man is walking his dog. They are growing old together.
The dog has learnt to walk like the man, or the man has been
    trained, by the dog,
to walk like him. The man's wife, who is waiting in the kitchen
on their third-floor walk-up, watching waves of coffee
flood the Bakelite dome of their percolator,
walks like the dog too. I once dated a Russian mass spectometrist
who said when he spoke to his akita, the akita spoke back.

EVERY PROMISE EVENTUALLY SOUNDS
LIKE AN APOLOGY

The truth is a misery of gas-station roses,
cellophane-haloed in a Quick Mix vase.
In the right light, anything can be beautiful.

It takes 63 days to form a habit, 32 hours
for someone's smell to leave the sheets, longer—
if you count the hotel room of the imagination.

The saint inside me is writing a new glossary of love.
The entry for *godliness* is missing.
Last summer, I resolved to give up meat,

not because I don't like the taste but to avoid
the bloody aftermath of flossing.
I dance the samba box-step with a selfie stick.

I paint my toenails Redemption Red.
The saint inside me is wringing her hands.
The truth is: of course the truth

has something to hide. I call a realtor
about a lie I can live with. He takes one look
at my pay stubs, says I'll never afford the rent.

BOY GEORGE IS MY SPIRIT ANIMAL
(after Morgan Parker)

I have always been free without conditions.
There are few limits to what I'll do.
Sometimes I fuck strangers because I want them
to feel beautiful. Death leaves notes under my dreams:
Skadoodle your boodle, honey, you're not a kid anymore.
I'm afraid of her because she seems so lonely.
7-Eleven is heaven. The cashiers are angels.
At night, I drink a lot of wine, and most nights
when I drink, scars fall out of my mouth
like monsoon moon songs. My doctor says
If we were in France, we wouldn't be having this conversation.
There's a man in the waiting room.
I want to kiss him, in case he has forgotten
he is beautiful. I have always been free
without conditions. My mother worries I'm a slut. She says
Every time you sleep with someone you lose part of your soul.
My soul is full of Four Roses bourbon.
When I think about perfection I think of lazy-eyed Usman,
the 7-Eleven cashier. Also, Nick, the neighborhood alcoholic.
Also, the empty nip bottles he tosses in our front yard.
We all volunteer to hold the heroin babies,
their Fornasetti eyes deep and wide as spoons.
I want to be beautiful. I want a bronzer for my aura.
The body I ordered is out of stock. People say contouring
and I hear contorting. They say cleavage and cheek bones
and cellulite city. Does everyone think I have nothing
to hide. I tongue the earlobe of an older white woman
to remind myself I'm not invisible. My mother is nearly invisible.
She is happy when I'm thin enough to fit into her jeans.
My skin means something. My mouth is good company.

I heart my mother, I do. Will I always be free without conditions.
What is there to lose. Boy beautiful George.
When I think about happiness I think of the weight
of the bodies we've been lent. Also, my father's affairs.
Yes, I am always asking for it. Lipstick sorrow shimmering.

THE PILLOW BOOK

The woman writes . . .

Things That Disturb:
Cinnamon whisky;
Orphaned pianos;
Gratuitous whistling

On the bodies of her lovers:

Things that Make the
Heart Beat Faster:
Cigarette before;
Cigarette after;
His breath in my throat

Like Sei Shônogon, she prepares . . .

Dangerous Things:
Advice of the flesh;
Listening to Portishead before
breakfast;
Collar bone or wrist

As paper, their skin:

Things That Ignite the
Senses:
Eileen dahlia;
Skin salt;
Sea urchin slathered on hot
bread

Wets the brush between . . .

Shameful Things:
That private moment;
Flattery during an eclipse;
Forgetting the smell of a past
lover

Her lips before it takes the ink:

Things Not to Be Trusted:
Air fresheners;

Logic of seduction;
Kissing without tongue

The woman uses them for . . .   Pleasurable Things:
Airmail paper;
Foreplay in sign language;
Hand on my back, in my hair

Whatever she wants. I want: Things That Make the
Heart Beat Fastest:
Wolf moon;
Dialect of glances;
Your breath in my throat again

BECAUSE I AM STUCK IN MY OWN SYNTAX

I dreamt I dreamed I had a conversation with the sea.
The waves did all the talking. They spoke Russian, I think.
The minute the test was over I forgot everything.

Science says music is the only memory
our bodies don't erase. Remember that piano
on the side of the street? Remember how I was crying?

Yes or no questions are disturbing in the way
empty ice-cube trays are disturbing because either choice
is a subtraction. I prefer additions.

Look at this new constellation I built. In it, we can go
hang gliding and wave at all the little villages
we never visited. Look how cute and faraway they seem.

I wanted to tell the sea there's more than one way
to skin a seal but I couldn't find a good translation.
Abstract is not the painting. Abstract is the crowd

gathered around the painting. Science says
my blue is not the same as yours. The beach was quiet
except for the vowels lingering like sea foam.

In this room, all the windows are open-
ended questions. I remember the vodka, how it was
always warm, how we drank it nice and slow.

THE LOVEMAKING HABITS OF ICEBERGS

Maybe there's nothing to learn
from the Dictionary of Sorrow,
no new words to describe a daffodil,
undressed by a shrug of wind.
Perhaps not every galaxy wonders
if it picked the right constellation.
Do you believe in destiny?
Don't roll your eyes; it's a fair question.
Persistence is to resilience what discretion
is to deception—in other words,
some people never find what they're looking for.
When an iceberg falls in love, the tectonic plates get nervous.
When two icebergs kiss, the gods start pacing.
Look at the sea. Most waves, no matter how hard
they break, never reach the shore.

MY DESIRE IS AN ORCHESTRA THAT ONLY KNOWS ONE SONG

Sometimes it's tone-deaf, often lacking rhythm.
My instruments, even the snare drum, are tuned
to innuendo. Contrary to popular belief,
there's no connection between the words
maestro and *maelstrom,* though gods
compose soundtracks to accompany every storm.

A one-man band is a meteor shower
everyone forgets to watch. Duos never sleep
through their alarms. The prime minister of Italy
keeps two pianos in his den. Do you know what I'm saying?
Musicians who play by ear might be talented
but they can rarely account for the whereabouts of their hands.

If you think I'm making excuses, consider Bartok's
Concerto for Orchestra, how seduction lingers
like a shroud of rain across a sultry afternoon.
I have talents. My hips are notorious.
I love the hollow forest of woodwinds, I do.
Most of my symphonies begin with an overture,

and end with an usher sweeping wrappers off the floor.

KISS ME AND YOU WILL SEE HOW
IMPORTANT YOU ARE

I needed a waltz in a minefield but I also needed you.
We could have gone foraging for planets together.
An egg-shaped moon is cracking the sky's skin

and I think we should talk—the way *silence*
in Braille feels like tracing my thumb
across the waking rows of your teeth,

or how touching a thought, even an uneven one,
is a bad idea because they bruise so easily.
Ailing is the star, ailing the start, auditioning

for another cameo. The hungering dog wails
through the long-legged afternoon.
What shape is made when *yes* tumbles

from the mouth of my volcano?
Why does what we want fail so differently
from what we know we should do?

Night's slow seduction is bound to pale.
We are still not dancing.
I'll give you these plug-in geraniums but save me

a fistful too. Here are my hieroglyphs:
untangle them. There goes a nebula
blown in half. When you read your biography,

know my hands are sorry for misquoting you.
This is the scene in the movie
where the cowgirl lassos her own heart.

That love remains a hypothesis,
a leaped-over landmine. Our shadows
prove light still fevers in the dark.

THE MONDEGREEN

To forever traipse the *vast*
in *devastation,* there is no choice.
The world's best ventriloquist
can't lie without twitching his ears.
Someone asks for a signature
when we wish they wanted an autograph.
All sequel long, the windchimes protesting.
How painstaking my pursuit
of the perfect avocado. How instantly
I forgot your name the moment
we were introduced. Hesitating
is the orgasm, evergreen every scar.
By the time I'd had enough to drink
the DJ kiboshed the wedding. Pawn shop
funeral urn, mutinous Skittle
in a velodrome, breathless love
on an inflatable bed. To be in downward dog
and realize I never knew your birthday.
The body's keenest memory
is its sense of smell. To spill
a phone number on a cocktail napkin.
To hike solo across hindsight's tundra
and to never, not once, play dead.

A NEW *NEW GUIDE* TO IRONY

Look at this chapel. It stands next to Casa Mingo,
the oldest cider house in Madrid.
The cider house is now a restaurant
famed for its roasted chicken.
One sits at the wooden trestle tables
wresting flesh from bone, while Goya's ghost
waves frantically from the chapel's steeple.

THE JANUARY OF HAVING EVERYTHING

For my fortieth birthday, I've asked the gods
for antlers. Every day I check the mirror for signs.

Even the quarrel of sparrows, navigating
the fire escape's snowmelt,

agrees I'm asking for a lesser miracle.
Velvet is trending this year. So is motherhood.

Don't you think I'd look great with antlers?
When I ask my lover this question, his teeth loosen.

Have you ever wondered what your head
gambled away when your heart wasn't looking?

A giraffe has small ossicones but a deliverance
of neck; elephants, blessed with ivory,

are inconsolable. Last night I dreamed I was
a white-tailed deer stuck on the median of Interstate 45,

traffic suicidal in both directions. Night loves
a good conundrum. If the gods ask,

I'll offer my left pinkie toe, a year without bourbon,
I'll agree to ten—no, twenty—extra pounds.

To feel the wind lick my velvet branches,
my lover's cheek listening for their pulse.

THE PERSUASION

Though my list of terrible ways to die keeps growing,
I'm really not a morbid person. I might have dreamed
my dog was hit by a car/devoured by
wolves/hit by a car but some therapists say it's healthy
to be proactive when it comes to grief.
Every now and then, I walk around the house
with my left eye duct-taped shut.
Yesterday, I put on a pale-pink Victoria's Secret negligee
and practiced voguing in front of the hallway mirror.
It's probably terrible to die never having seen
a shooting star. At least as bad, I'm guessing, to go
without deleting those Tinder accounts.
Do you think, with enough rehearsal, it's possible
to persuade even the most stubborn sadnesses?
A friend's pregnancy. A "roman" nose.
The toothbrush he left in the bathroom cabinet.
To imagine the worst-case scenario is to set all the clocks
ten minutes fast. It's the teaspoon of dirt I add to my coffee
to become accustomed to the taste.

THE ACCIDENT

In this movie, the most important angel
is impaled on a blade of grass.
Someone makes a speech,
and someone else pretends to be interested.
Every angel's aura is accompanied
by an aging maestro. Finding a realistic
stunt double, therefore, is nearly impossible.
The most important angel was taller
and more ambitious than the others.
Someone points at a roof window
and yells *skylight*. Someone else draws
a sky light and whispers *moon*.
Just because we ignore the subtitles doesn't mean
we won't eventually understand each other.
We wear our faces very, very carefully.

SURE, I TOOK THE PAMPHLET ON
BREAKING BAD HABITS

I need as much help as you do. Autocorrect insists
on turning my hugs and kisses into *oxen,*
and predictive text thinks my infidelities are *infinite.*
We all want to be there the moment the sun
kicks off its shoes, want the wild ones
to eat from our hands—who hasn't imagined their own
magnificent funeral? New Year's resolutions are exercises
in reflexive disappointment. In Greek, there are six
different words for *love,* and *fireworking* is a verb.
Does your heart have unpaid speeding tickets too?
I think it was Pissarro who said the definition of Monet
is painting the same haystack over and over and expecting
a different result. This can be applied to the odds
of winning the lottery but not to lightning's striking
sense of smell. Siddhartha sat under the bodhi tree
for seven weeks waiting for enlightenment.
Longer than it takes a dull pencil to annul a marriage.
Longer than it takes flirtation to round the corner of betrayal.

CHARADES

It's not that Egon Schiele didn't appreciate
the sunrise of peaches on the kitchen table,
flesh so ripe it broke the day's skin—

hands, like muses, are accustomed to duplicity:
heading out the door each day in the same direction,
one doing the work of saints, and the other,

well, the other prefers not to talk about it.
The word *omnifarious* means *everywhere*
but sounds like the slow seep of trouble

from a leaky sink. When the sky sleeps,
clouds secretly study the language of flight.
The snow pigeon breaks her lover's wings

before mating. Sometimes the ocean holds its breath
long enough to invent a new shade of blue.
Who doesn't think they'll be the hero

who wrestles the lid from the jar?
The *Mona Lisa* is only 21 inches wide,
smaller than a pillowcase, shorter

than a horse's tail brushing away
a fly. She was sleeping with the groundskeeper
but that's a different story.

To define *frigorific* as *freezing*
is to forget the pleasure of a cartwheel.
This milk's gone sour—taste it.

IN FLAGRANTE

At this juncture, I'd like to revise my defense:
Takis Fuego, a latent talent for anagrams,
the time when I was seven and my grandmother
caught me handing a love letter to the electrician.
Hello, Shame, it's nice to finally meet you.
When I'm feeling low-aerialist, I watch YouTube tutorials
on how to unlock handcuffs with your tongue.
Something very beautiful is at the epicenter
of this indictment: an unflappable trembling
of finches, for example, my leopard-print jeans.
Nobody wants waffles for breakfast but here I am,
firing the pan up anyway. This has always been my problem.
Metaphors are notoriously reliable witnesses.
My aliases are also notorious but for reasons
we probably shouldn't discuss here. Uncuff me,
and I'll do that thing you like with my hands.
Probable cause: 98% synth-pop and 2% predilection.
It's easy to marvel at the stars because they're so far away.

A NEW *NEW GUIDE* TO ROOT VEGETABLES

Apparently, some men have walked on the moon.
I wonder what it smelled like up there.
I wonder if Neil, walking around the farmer's market
on a crisp Sunday morning, beagle's leash in one hand,
wife's purse in the other, paused by a rutabaga
or a bunch of parsnips, and said,
Carol, this is it! I haven't smelled the moon in years!

MUTUAL DISAMBIGUATION

I wish my antimatter had grown up
to be normal matter. It's like feeling sad

for the faceted Swarovski crystal
on the Disney bracelet at the Dollar Store.

It's like drinking the Cherry Pucker anyway.
Why does the past always introduce itself

after it's already too late?—Hello, Lapsed Ovaries;
Nice to Meet You, Ex-Señor Right.

Every day my heart lines up
to ride the zip line between rapture and pain.

What if you wore a tartan kilt
and black Doc Marten boots? What if sex was more

than a means of making weather? One ex-husband,
no kids. I can guess what you're thinking.

This could be the part where I unspool my antiparticles
and crash them into yours anyway.

Have you ever witnessed the exact moment the moon
punches a hole in the forgery of night?

IN OUR GARDEN OF EDEN

There was no apple; or if there was, and the apple was to blame,
there were many of them, a thousand, it seemed, flush-cheeked
suns, strung like lanterns across the horizon
of our minds' eye, lit, as if galvanized, iron-hot at their cores,
and burning: even in the rage of darkness, in the dream
that would eventually befall us. Beyond the unkindness
of ravens dimming the garden's edge, above, or maybe below
their shadow, a desert, vast as our emptiness, unfolded.
We wrote our names in the ochre dust and waited.
We watched the sifting dunes hunger away their sand.
If there was a hunger, had we sated it? Father, please forgive us,
but in our Garden of Eden there was no snake, none
except the sweet-bitter mist that fell across our skin at dawn,
and the smell of it after, rising, as if from inside us, warm
like breath ascending the coils of an electric afternoon.
Father, You call it *malum,* but that's not the apple we tasted.

THE PROPHECY

A snow leopard never sees its own reflection.
This is one way to use *tragic* in a sentence.
Another is to remember Beethoven never heard
the applause of rain. Some people say the Greeks
invented tragedy but it was really the gods,
the moment they turned the lights on.
My heart is a 24-hour convenience store.
Its prophecy is a game of telephone.
Between what I've done and what I've failed to do,
regret's pendulum faithfully swings.
When Eve swore she wouldn't eat the apple,
did she account for pleasure—the lilt and tremble
of bees dancing, scales shimmying
against her skin? Chafing the shoulder blades
of all my promises: a pair of incipient wings.

PLEASE DON'T LEAVE ME UNATTENDED

I noticed, last night, browsing Casual Encounters on Craigslist,
two cherry trees across the street are blooming.

M4w, w4w . . . It's true, I suppose, I am no stranger to sex
with strangers—except, define: *stranger.*

December in New England, two trees in bloom:
if asked, I could fall in love with you in an instant.

Should it come down to a confession,
the kind that almost changes things,

like a dream so unspeakably real
and because so real, then shameful,

I would say *Yesterday, the night was so pale*
I could barely distinguish the blossoms from the sky.

And the body? I'm afraid it doesn't know what it wants,
and by this, I mean it wants everything.

But none of this explains why those two trees
are flowering out of season. None of this explains

the difference between *nature* and *natural,*
if there is a difference, however slight.

HOW TO LOVE EVERYONE AND
ALMOST GET AWAY WITH IT

I always thought a wolverine was some smaller version of a wolf.
I was wrong about that. I was wrong to rely on envelopes
as synonyms for surprise, sunrise as shorthand
for peaches; wrong to expect my damage
wouldn't be permanent. After an outburst of silence, we arrive
at a place where the landscape is best appreciated
with our eyes closed. I have been a devout
acrobat but I'm learning to look less flexible.
Can you tell the difference between a guinea pig and a hamster?
There are two ways to interpret that question.
Sometimes I kiss my male friends on the lips.
Sometimes I kiss the straight ones
on the sides of their mouths, and we both know
what I'm doing. Someone says, *Don't drink all the oyster liquor!*
I'm so thirsty I leave the bathroom light on all night
but when brushing my teeth, I never keep the faucet running.
I'm so hungry I devour duplicity. Being a person with loose ethics
has its benefits—the lotus position, for example, a mantra of
    ankle boots.
Taxonomy is a trick, like pulling a rabbit out of a hat.
Or sometimes a hare. Maybe I was wrong to say I loved you,
even if it was true. Here are my translations: recycle them.
Here is my karaoke heart. We still don't agree
whether the color periwinkle swings purple
or leans more blue. Nonetheless, innuendo. Nonetheless,
I'd gladly spend the afternoon revising my misdemeanors with you.

A NEW *NEW GUIDE* TO ENTROPY

In this film, a woman practices the art of calligraphy
on her lovers' skin. Nagiko is not always pleased with them:
too oily, too dry, too much hair, too wrinkled.
Then she meets Jerome, whose skin (and everything else),
until he meets his tragic end, is perfect. I have often wondered
why we bury or burn our dead. For those who die young,
or whose beauty has not yet abandoned them,
there ought to be something more.

WE ALL GET TURNED AROUND

This game requires audio, compulsory
tears, peach pits, roadkill, the occasional
orgasm. At the halfway mark, the fairy tales
all need tourniquets. Try as I might to ignore
my imagination, desire pulls up a chair
and bangs her fists on the table.
A rose is just a rose, despite the impulse
to bleed every thorn symbolic;
there's always a third date brazen enough
to steal the restaurant forks; in each landfill:
a perfectly good piano. Who put the *end*
in *crescendo,* the *over* in *lover?*
Poor Van Gogh, all those sunflowers and still,
terror. The bride marries anyway,
something her mother says
about the devil you know. In the corner
of the operating room, a fire extinguisher,
waiting to explode its inner heroine.
Dusk throws the dice. The horizon
sees the bet and raises. This game
requires mouthguards, voluntary grief,
Allen wrenches, ashtrays, the occasional
obsession. Take the evacuation route:
I have loved as indiscriminately as an avalanche.
Someone says *kaleidoscope* when they mean
horoscope. We all get turned around.

IN MY WANDERING CIRCUS OF DESIRE

I am in the habit
        of daring men I meet
                to try their feet at funambulism.
A feverish applause of clouds
           loiters each night above.
                 Close your eyes, I say,
if you're afraid of falling.
           Danger is a detour, my imagination's
trespass. I should stop
        conjuring your unmapped body
              right before bed.
Suspended in the dream light
          of a sharpening hangnail moon,
    a sign says: *Welcome Back, Desolation.*
               Tiny lies
grip my tongue
        like the legs of expensive bourbon.
I have not been, I am mostly
           good.   I dare you
    to love me—
          my tripwire heart—
Watch the lions devour
        snatch it right off my sleeve.

VANISHING POINTS OF ARRIVAL

Sometimes you want to love someone
and it's the worst kind of loneliness. A silver spill
of effort at the planetarium. A graveyard of stars.

Outside the hotel I called my mother and the truth
was almost vertical. It's impossible to fill
an empty box. I had a thought like that.

I had an idea of myself that wasn't translatable.
To be naked with an indifferent itinerary.
To touch a man to sleep while the skyline

jags like an echocardiogram. What tenderer
crater could I have given him? Both nights
he called his kid. At the airport bar, it was just me

and a woman with her canary. Chablis levity.
He wouldn't translate me. Misnomer
of safety pins holding my face together.

SANGUINE

And yet, united as we were, we had never been so alone.
—Randolph Stow

And now,
the bull is entering
the ring, and the ring,
for a moment, adores it.

Around us,
         the ebullient crowd is divided,

sun seats and, more desirable,
those in the shade, as the shadow
of the cape on the darkening ground
edges the world forward a little,
and the difference, between what is cast
and cast upon, seems indistinguishable.

The bull is wounded.
Who knows if loss
is always a symptom of pain?
         Tenderness
in the distance. Above us
an affection of clouds.
The one with the cape
bending and unbending,

bowing, as if to say,
         damage,
as understood when one life
swells onto the shore of another,
might be a flexing of the same muscle that,
upon autopsy, turns out to have been
desire all along.

The bull is bleeding but does not back away.
What I've called my heart almost acts like one.

SWEET GIRL

Tell them about the night he lights candles
          and kisses your back with wax.
     How it's your first lesson, and only he speaks, and the night
         is like a field of horses where someone has a carrot
but you're unsure who. Tell them what you know
        about dismemberment.
   The night is a field is a body he makes you own,
   the cannibal inside your head saying
      It's not that you don't want it, Sweet Girl,
        you just imagined it differently.

So what if it is a sad story? Tell them
       about the feeling that comes after,
   the surprise of blood in your skirt, how the first night
      he's an experiment in resilience.
Hand where he puts it, mouth,
     gift of damage
beneath your high school uniform.
     And you want to learn the lesson, you do.
So tell them, instead, about the night your body is an avatar
          not addicted to tenderness, where the
       horses,
   startled into flight, run, until they finish quartering,
   in which the man among them does not say
     Leave, please, before I rape you and later,
    later,
       Sweet Girl, are you all right?

A NEW *NEW GUIDE* TO SELF-HELP

This actor is the protagonist of a terrible tragedy.
He is using the Stanislavsky technique to play the part.
Right before the third act, the director instructs him to cry.
The actor tries to remember a time in his life
when he had the blues so bad he was almost broken,
but he thinks of nothing. In that moment, the actor realizes
he has not truly lived, and is overwhelmed by sadness.
He uses this method every night in a sold-out show.

WEAPONS OF PROBABLE DESTRUCTION

One must know a member of the organization
to receive an invitation. Please explain
the rules to me again. Thirteen is an unlucky number
but I don't know why. There is only one window
in the house from which to observe the blush
of sunrise, and it is disconcerting to realize, given
the magnitude of the event, how many times
I have missed it by looking in the wrong direction.

NPR reports: The president has ordered men with HIV
to rape the women of the families who want to vote against him.
I am looking at a reproduction of a Schiele painting:
the dark-haired man in the red loincloth, one talon
perched across his forehead, the other twisted below his chin.
Emaciated. Most days, I would like to be more angular.
A realtor on HGTV shows a couple the "master" bedroom.
Someone is sending a message.

Last year I went to Sri Lanka. I spent ten days on the beach
in Tangalle where the air smelled of sea salt and drying fish.
From a distance, the ocean looked Marlboro Country blue.
I used to think ignoring the color of a person's skin
was the best way to avoid being racist. This, I discovered,
is the same as pretending everyone is white. The difference
between black magic and white magic is associative:
a black cat is a sign of bad luck; a white lie, not as bad.

NPR reports: He is gassing his own people. I don't know
who my people are; do you? By this, I mean, are there others
I am under less of an obligation to care about?
The residents of Del Rio, Texas, have more in common
with the citizens of Ciudad Acuña but they are separated
by an international border, a line in the sand.
The Dalai Lama advised the monks not to fight back.

HAVING SAID THAT

Maybe starlight is tired of trying to outshine the moon,
and the cat deserves an apology for what he's had to see.
Maybe every heart needs a pair of sensible shoes.

Imagine being an astronaut. Worst-case scenario
we'd float for an infinity together, dead,
but forever thirty-three. The problem, I've learned,

with musical chairs is the winner ends up lonely.
Good intentions are like painkillers, you only need them
when it already hurts. If I seem distracted,

it's probably because your cologne reminds me
of a blaze of snapdragons on the breath of bloom.
Does it still count as betrayal if we just imagine kissing?

I have had impure thoughts about angels.
I have had impure thoughts about you.
Also, I have no idea how electricity works

and I never check my bank statements.
Of the seven deadly sins, Lust is the best dancer,
though sometimes her outfits are inappropriate.

Am I being inappropriate? It's not easy being the margarita
that gives everyone a hangover. Given their violence,
most fairy tales should be rated NC-17.

TELL ME THE ONE ABOUT THE MARXIST
WITH A HORSE NAMED TROTSKY

Never mind the world is a carousel,
its axis tilted; how we spin with it,

leaning toward some greater spark—
funhouse reflections, the sun-ripened apricots

suspended in Grandmother's bottle of schnapps,
too keen for comfort, the husky mix

who hears electricity's tango with the walls—
nothing should shock you.

It's true, the stars keep their distance.
Then again, their light has been dead for years.

When it comes to tragedy, I'm no oracle;
I'd like to be a confident nude,

less open to suggestion, but let's face it:
there are at least ten different species

of cloud, and I can't spell any of them.
Any bartender will tell you, most people

would rather undress their secrets
with a stranger than a friend. Jesus and Lazarus

were once strangers. You and I are strangers.
Activities common among strangers

include killing or reviving or having sex
with each other. Whose hand touched you last?

Would you recognize it in a lineup, would you recognize
your own? You don't have to believe in fate to agree

it only takes one person to derange another's orbit,
for better or worse, and mostly without ceremony.

At every longitude: a place where trouble's
been buried. A koala's fingerprints are so close

to a human's, they've occasionally been confused
at the scene of a crime.

DELIVERY BY MOUTH

Most weeks I'm accordion but I'd prefer to be harmonica.
My body language is easier to read with the lights turned off.
Accord and harmony are synonyms
for the parts of speech that leave a lump in my throat.
At the dinner party someone says
Sorry for all this talk about pregnancy.
Wolves are in the water. Wolves are in the water
so the water better learn how to swim.

Sometimes my dreams are magic acts where everyone
ends up naked. No one loves a good seduction more than me.
Don't worry. My tragedy is unsinkable, and I still
have plenty of tickets. At what age is it too late
to take up piano? A dream is both a noun and a verb,
a skylight in a nightclub, an orgasm on buttered toast.
Here are my sequins: catch them. Here is my fender-bender

heart. Last night I dreamed I delivered
a stillborn by mouth. I'm more or less as happy as you.

THE FLIGHTLESS BIRDS

Then, as if silence is the sound one heart makes
when it turns away from another, we agreed to it.
There wasn't any fire into which we could pitch
our grief; no shrine erected in our memory—
the sky remained closed for renovations.
Of the intelligence of clouds, I know, you were certain.
Look at the ocean. There was a time when desire
swelled beneath us, and so, buoyed by our weightlessness,
I thought we could fly. No, that isn't right.
More like a starfish that, having accepted dismemberment,
knows every torn limb eventually grows back.
I don't believe the stories the others told you,
tales of scaling the summits of unmet expectations,
of nesting in the eaves of stars—
Look, the ground is bristling with kindnesses.
Every flower I plant blooms with envy;
the bloodworms taste fat and succulent as dreams.

BECAUSE THERE'S NO EMOJI FOR MEMORY

Maybe I'll forget the blue hydrangeas
        I was promised,
           the stoplight foreplay
at the junction of Hollywood and Vine,
even erase the insult of having been the only one
        still awake at midnight.
Forget the emojis.
Fuck Björk.
        Why do dappled bands of color
      appear in the tiny oil slicks
that drift across puddles on a rainy day?
      Isn't it sad that some loves
           are better on paper?
In our hotel room, his Saran-wrapped
        orange nesting on the nightstand,
he showed me how to write my name
      in two foreign languages.
          Why does the past
      sleep with us when we hope
the person beside us is the future?
      I was always three drinks ahead of him.
      He said my *cuaderno* was beautiful.
We both agreed the bathroom
        was too close to the bed.

APPASSIONATA SONATA & OTHER WORKS
FOR SOLO PIANO

Say *trip the light fantastic* three times
before you shave that five o'clock shadow.
I like my men with facial hair.
The day is spilling its hope like tequila
in the hands of a less experienced woman.
Don't worry about the bats circling the apricot tree,
the piranhas pirating the river—take my hunger
as a compliment. I know how you want it.

If I ink an anatomical heart
on my inner thigh, will you quit smoking?
If it makes you more comfortable,
I'll put my underwear back on right after sex.
Are you sure you don't want another beer?
In the malty haze that settles over the city at dusk,
it's hard to see me. Maybe one day, it'll be true
when I say *Nobody knows you like me.*

DEATH MASK 23

Having looked closer at the painting,
I don't agree. You say you'd recognize
that kind of relief anywhere—

eyes still, fist finally unfurled, mouth
abandoning its creases—you, knowing a thing or two
about submission. Look outside.

Snow is turning the world into TV static,
but just this morning, the sky
was blue enough to swim in. It's easy

to mistake my empty wineglass
for resolve, to call the picked hibiscus
release, easy to imagine

the moment before all unraveling
as some kind of glory.
But I don't agree. The snowflakes

are larger now, their weight
means the storm is ending. Look again.
The angle of the neck, lurch of chin,

Adam's apple wrenching the throat.
Torment is here, my love. Tell me again
what you know about holding on.

DON'T STAY, DON'T GO

It's impossible to know
        why the horse
   stood so close to the fire.
Impossible, really, to guess
    if it felt the approaching heat
    or if the smoke, entering
        aimless as moss,
   was first.
You were in my dream again last night.
    You wore a thick
   leather jacket, the familiar smell
       of engine oil
    still slick in its trenches.
   I have often wondered if there's such a thing
      as a moment that makes all the difference.
   And if such a moment exists,
      why it so often insists
     on lying down with all the others,
  impossible to tell, then,
       who's sleeping
    and who's playing dead.
Maybe the horse
    was tethered
   to an idea of itself that, in the end,
it couldn't resist. The way a door
   closes,
      either toward or
   away from you, depending
on where you stand.

A NEW *NEW GUIDE* TO HUSBANDRY

On the 13th of June every year
young women come to the chapel of Saint Anthony
to pray for a husband. For their part,
the husbands are elsewhere.
They are in a field catching lizards.

WHISTLING DIXIE

The storm wishes it were more like a metronome,
and the abacus is envious of the squall.
Same old story. The impresario confuses foxtrot
with foxglove, and bingo: *danse macabre.*
Everywhere desire is detonating fuchsias,
while the alarm clock inside of me
is again startled by its own machinery.
Look at this perfect instrument
I've never learned to play. When I meet you, song,
why are you always in such a hurry?
Someone should do something about those fire ants.
Unshackle this trapeze. Commemorate
my compulsions. I like it when restaurants
put my leftovers in tin foil
shaped like a swan. My smokestack lungs
can still whistle a dixie or two. To an oyster,
the wave's lash feels like flocked velvet,
so there's that to consider. It's all fine dining
here in delirium. Every morning,
a lesser sin delivers half my heart
on a silver platter. The other half? Some cherub
has it stashed under his mattress with his porn.

MIXED MESSAGES

Don't get me wrong, I'm still not certain about anything.
The perils of helium, for example, my Tuesday shoes,
whether 'tis nobler to be steadily plaid
or sporadically sequin. Actions followed by words.
Or is it the other way around? In this casino,
we do not take kindly to horoscopes.
You know how right after something really bad
or really good happens, people cover their mouths,
and make a noise like the lighting of a Bunsen flame?
Some say the hand is to stop the soul escaping.
I haven't heard an explanation for the sound.
The billboard reads *Your best self is right around this corner!*
To be certain, and to be right, are different skylines
in the same city. Someone throw me that bouquet.
I'll try not to blow up this perfect experiment
but I can't make any promises. In canasta,
the jokers are the highest-scoring cards.

PLASTICITY THEORY

I used to think if I poked my eye out often enough,
I'd eventually grow a second heart.
A second heart would have its advantages,
the extra storage, of course, and space
for guests to stay when they came to visit.
Don't you think it's strange a bird's first instinct
is to attack its own reflection?
Stranger, still, that heaven and hell
were created by an angel who never learned how to fly.
My one good eye can read trouble's shopping list
from a distance of thirteen feet.
My one good eye is a snow globe
where tourists forget their sadness
by rubbing two sticks together.
I used to think my second heart
would be the world's loudest greenhouse.
I used to think desire had a small carbon footprint.
We touch the thing in front of us.
We either blow or break the glass.

BLOOM BOX ODE

Surely Mondrian was roused, at least once,
by the arc of a gibbous moon. You go your whole life
without reading the safety card provided
in the front seat pocket. All summer long, the rosebush
is deafening. How lucky to be the koi afloat
in the sunken garden, to be the ring of fire
boiling the pot of stew. I've failed every test
but here I am, in charge of this contraption.
Paperweights are shiftless, lightning precocious.
Instinctively, our eyes adjust to the dark.
If the diamond mine closes we'll still have
this jackhammer. We can excavate that AC/DC cassette
and someone will call us god. No one expects
the ordinary. Your American Beauty was deafening.
Oh, poor desire, rattling the serpent's throat.

POEM BEGINNING WITH A SENTENCE
BY DEAN YOUNG

Part of me still believes
it's possible to breathe
fire. Believes in the healing powers
of the accordion.
Yesterday, I eavesdropped
on an old couple in the doctor's waiting room
and when she asked for the time
it was as if her beloved held
all the world's sundials
between the trembling sky
of his hands. That the sky will always
be trembling, yes, I believe that too.
I'm not the first person
to press my ear to a radiator
and swear to hear God whistling the tune
of Miles Davis's "All Blues."
Not the last person to ask if suffering's meter
ever stops ticking over.
Maybe it's better to be the bowed
sword of bamboo than the sickle,
to be the dancefloor's lone survivor,
wearing morning's dampening crown.
Once, I performed twenty-three pushups
and called it a lesson in survival.
Once, I left a man I loved
which was also a lesson
but in what, I'm still not sure.
Part of me believes it's possible
to measure an apology's temperature
by holding it over warm breath.
This thought of you like smoke
riding the hooked cursive of the wind.

A NEW *NEW GUIDE* TO MOBILITY

Two trains leave the station at the same time.
One is a luxury express. Its seats are upholstered
with full-grain leather, the kind that smells of
spice box and pine, and its dining car,
open day and night, serves crustless tea sandwiches
and real French champagne. The other is a slow-going
freight train. It has a small cramped car for passengers
who purchase their tickets at a discounted fee,
and along the way makes several stops, hefting
goods onto and from its wagons.
Though both trains arrive at the same destination,
it is unlikely they'll ever pass each other.

SOUVENIR

I feed my wolf nostalgia but then what?
He's already obsessed with the lunar tides.
He's digging up the yard again, fixed
on burying night's roving silver eye.
Read *Twenty Love Poems and a Song of Despair*
often enough and, like me, you'll find yourself
rummaging memory's junk drawer,
excavating some old anchor, some twilight-blackened
scrap of hull. You call that a heart?
I call it a basement with plenty of storage.
Though no one says we have to choose
just one healing crystal from the souvenir shop,
fate's twenty-one flavors eventually melt.
You get on the plane or you don't—
either way, someone's hemorrhaging.
What if nostalgia's nothing more than regret
wearing full-coverage foundation?
The prom dress in my closet thinks it's still 1984.
To throw away the fortune cookies
with the plum sauce. To miss what I could have had
but lost. Quiet for once with the moon
in his mouth, my wolf yells: *Hey! Time for breakfast!*
I scavenge the wreckage of sunrise
like it's a busted piñata. I wish I could remember
why I never bought that rock.

COIN-TOSS THEORIES

Gravity and the sky are arguing again
about who needs the other more.
Truth is usually a hung jury.

I see a bat—no, a submarine—
in the inkblot; you see two people kissing.
Any good mathematician can predict the odds

of running into our best selves
in the frozen-food aisle, but the probability of a heart
landing predator- or prey-side up

remains unforeseeable. Statistically speaking,
left-handed doctors are less likely
to give terminal diagnoses. Ambidextrous

psychologists, more likely to cross the line.
After every game of truth or dare,
someone leaves the room crying.

The gods changed their minds
nineteen times today;
how many times have you?

In the sixteenth century, the Catholic church
appointed a devil's advocate who proved,
if you dig deep enough, most saints have flaws.

The definition of *horizon* depends on where the sky
reaches its limits, on whether they believe
my side of the story, or if they believe yours.

ALL SUCH INTIMACIES

By now I thought I'd be able
to tell this asteroid and this comet apart.
I suppose you've already noticed,
I generally excel at nuance.
In a glance, I can distinguish between
the thirty-nine frowns of contrition.
I practice each of them
in the bathroom mirror every morning.
When an asteroid braces for impact
it closes its mouth and imagines the sound
of snow striking an outstretched tongue.
So do I. All such intimacies
require hydrogen, oxygen, and a straitjacket.
If you stare long enough at an open flame
your eyes start to water.
Some people might mistake your resolve
for tears. Once, I mistook an aardvark
for an armadillo. I threw it on its back
and expected it to furl into a ball.
Isn't the end of anything always limping,
dragging its one good intention
across the finish line where a minor god waits
with a hoarse throat and a tepid beer?
A pregnant armadillo can gestate denial
for as long as eleven years.
A comet, I remember now, is mostly ice
though it often orbits too close to the sun.

POEM IN DEFENSE

Not every drowning sunset
can be rescued from the sea,
revived, returned to the horizon.
A single poppy can intoxicate a field.

Maybe you're right,
what I've done is unforgivable.

Thunder is the gods cracking their knuckles—
do I deserve a second chance
at walking up to the piano
and getting the lyrics right?

The half-life of a bad idea
is longer than the lifespan of an apology.
When a plant has a near-death experience
it produces flowers, hoping the species
will succeed. In Varanasi, failed loves
are thrown into the Ganges
where they're believed to enter the netherworld
of unborn promises.

Do you think it's true
the heart is susceptible
to the kind of damage that,
in the end, will turn out
to be irrevocable?

I thought I was trapped.
My wings were wild with panic.

A ship's captain fears the mutinous anchor
more than the eye of the raging storm.

KNOW THIS

You will be a believer in angels;
you will steal and then spend the rain;
you will be asked how you spent all the time

that has been given you; you will wish
this was the first of your elaborate stories.
You will always be willing to take off your clothes,

except in your own bedroom.
There will be an arrangement of loneliness
between the clouds and the sky.

In case of emergency, you will call
the angel who sold you a one-way ticket
to the most desolate place on earth. You will be

a believer of anything. You and Disaster
will drink too much tequila, and forget
where in the yard you buried your hearts.

WITH THESE WINGS

As you are waiting in line to buy tickets to the performance
of your ideal self, notice the sky. There is one species of cloud

whose outer limits look like a breadknife's serrated edge.
Just this morning you made a deal with a boxcutter.

Consider the animal ahead of you who is waiting to polish
his own beauty. Give him the alibi from your pocket

so he has something else to do with his hands.
If the crows circling the crude, wide blade try to cut in line,

imagine the burden of flight, of having failed when their mothers
sent them out into the world, saying *With these wings you can do
    anything.*

Ask for permission to touch their feathers.
The residue on your fingers will feel like empathy.

The suicides undress their wounds and, from them, the sky salts
    its feast.
That you have a singular purpose and have not yet found it

is reason enough. Some people claim if you crave the ecstatic
it will always feed you. Question this theory.

The animal behind you is luminous with hunger. Her hands
are broken mirrors. Notice the distinction between the ground

and the sky is softening. It's the wind undressing the branches.
It's your applause for waiting in a line that never ends.

NOTES

The "A New *New Guide*" sequence is in conversation with Kenneth Koch's "A New Guide," in *One Train* (New York: Knopf, 1994), 7–15.

"Drunkest Etc." is a response to Dean Young's "Drunker etc.," in *Bender: New and Selected Poems* (Port Townsend, WA: Copper Canyon Press, 2012), 54.

"The Pillow Book" was inspired by *The Pillow Book of Sei Shonagon*, trans. and ed. Ivan Morris (London: Penguin, 1967). Two of the list titles are borrowed or rephrased from that text: "Things That Make One's Heart Beat Faster" and "Shameful Things" (51, 144).

The title "Kiss Me and You Will See How Important You Are" is inspired by Sylvia Plath's line "Kiss me, and you will see how important I am," in *The Unabridged Journals of Sylvia Plath,* ed. Karen V. Kukil (New York: Anchor, 2000).

In "Know This," the sentence "You will be asked how you spent all the time that has been given to you" paraphrases " All the time that is given to thee, it shall be asked of thee how thou hast spent it, " in *The Cloud of Unknowing,* trans. Clifton Wolters (London: Penguin, 1961), 62.

ACKNOWLEDGMENTS

A multitude of thanks to the editors, readers, and staff members of the following publications, where these poems, sometimes in different form, first appeared:

American Journal of Poetry: "Weapons of Probable Destruction"
American Poetry Journal: "Sweet Girl"
Arts & Letters: "At Washington Square Tavern"
Barrow Street: "Boy George Is My Spirit Animal"
Florida Review: "In Our Garden of Eden"
Free State Review: "Driving Lessons," "How to Love Everyone and Almost Get Away with It"
Grist: "The Mondegreen"
Jabberwock Review: "Know This"
Jet Fuel Review: "The Bridge between Us," "The January of Having Everything," "S.O.S."
Lake Effect: "Having Said That," "Wanderlust"
Laurel Review: "Kiss Me and You Will See How Important You Are," "Mutual Disambiguation"
MAYDAY Magazine: "A New *New Guide*" sequence
New Ohio Review: "Another Version of My Confession"
Ninth Letter: "If You're Anything like Me"
Painted Bride Quarterly: "Drunkest Etc."
Pinch Journal: "Every Promise Eventually Sounds like an Apology," "The Lovemaking Habits of Icebergs"
Rabbit Catastrophe: "Museum of the Heart"
RHINO: "The Igneous Hours"
Salt Hill: "Because There's No Emoji for Memory"
Southerly: "The Flightless Birds"
Spillway: "Death Mask 23"
Washington Square Review: "Delivery by Mouth"
Zone 3: Eleven Days in Alicante
Verse Daily: "Because There's No Emoji for Memory"

My deepest thanks and gratitude go to the Warren Wilson MFA Program for Writers; to Ellen Bryant Voigt and Debra Allbery, who founded and sustain the magic; and to the Wally alumni, for their continued generosity and support. Without that program this book would not exist. To Alan Shapiro, James Longenbach, Maurice Manning, Roger Reeves, C. Dale Young, Scott Challener, and Reginald Dwayne Betts—my dear teachers. There aren't words to describe what you've given me. I hope you know how blessed I feel to have learned from you. I hope I always make you proud.

For their genius, unending thanks, too, to Rick Bursky and Barrett Warner. Thank you for your careful reading of these poems and for so often knowing what my poems needed before I did.

To Cynthia Gunadi, for everything: oxen forever.

For advice, encouragement, and stamina, I'm indebted to Joseph Capista, Asako "Sox" Serizawa, Maria Koundoura, Jennifer Sperry Steinorth, and Geoff Kronik. Thanks, too, to my friends and colleagues who have buoyed me on this journey and whose conversation inspired some of these poems: Jennifer Meek, Sahil Mehta, David Flaschenriem, Ed Burke, Moshe Elmekias, Cindy Morton Elmekias, Richard Wein, Brian Cummings, Fay Dillof, Peter Schireson, Tracy Winn, Helen Fremont, and Avra Elliot.

Many of these poems were written during THE GRIND. Thanks to Ross White and Noah Stetzer for nudging me each month and keeping THE GRIND rolling, and thanks to everyone who has shared in the delight/ torture with me these last few years.

For your abundant light, thank you Calvin Marcellus Braxton.

Thank you to judges Dara Wier, James Haug, Arda Collins, and Arisa White for selecting this book for the Juniper Prize, as well as to Courtney Andree, Sally Nichols, Rachael DeShano, Dawn Potter, and the University of Massachusetts Press for bringing these words to life. Thanks, as well, to Friends of Writers and the Massachusetts Cultural Council for their generosity that helped support this work.

For keeping the ship afloat, I owe much to my Estragon family. Thank you!

For cooking all those dinners, forgiving my absences, and believing in me, my greatest thanks and love go to my partner, Julio. Thank you, Camille. Thank you, Ines. Helga, Carol, Steve, David, and Matthew, thank you. Denmark, thank you for listening. To my parents, Jackie and Josef Egger: thank you for being the people I most admire, for giving me everything, and for loving me anyway. And to all the beauties everywhere—shine on, my loves, shine on.

JUNIPER
JUNIPER PRIZE FOR POETRY

This volume is the forty-eighth recipient of the
Juniper Prize for Poetry, established in 1975 by
University of Massachusetts Press in collaboration with
the UMass Amherst MFA program for Poets and Writers.
The prize is named in honor of the poet Robert Francis
(1901–1987), who for many years lived in Fort Juniper,
a tiny home of his own construction, in Amherst.